D0922730

COUNTRY
WITHOUT
MAPS

COUNTRY
WITHOUT
MAPS

Jean Garrigue

The Macmillan Company, New York

Collier-Macmillan Limited, London

First printing

The Macmillan Company, New York
Collier-Macmillan Canada Ltd., Toronto, Ontario

Library of Congress catalog card number: 64–22600

DESIGNED BY MARY A. BROWN
Printed in the United States of America

Acknowledgments

Some of these poems were originally published in *The Paris Review, Poets and
the Past, Poetry Northwest, The New Republic, The Virginia Quarterly Review,
The American Scholar, The Literary Review, Kenyon Review, The Transatlantic
Review, Prism, December,* and *Voices.* The poems "Cortège for Colette" and
"Amsterdam Letter"—1960; "They Guided Birds" (originally published under the
title "Of History More Like Myth")—1963; and "A Note to La Fontaine"—1964;
copyrighted © by The New Yorker Magazine, Inc. in the respective years shown.
"Spring Song II" (originally published under the title "Song II"), "Remember
That Country" (originally published under the title "Of Provence and the River
Var"), "How I Loved," "On the Legends of a Dancer," "Her Spring Song," "The
Adam Tree," " 'When Shall We Set Sail For Happiness?'," "French Country
Circus," were first published in *Poetry.* The following poems originally appeared
in *The Hudson Review:* "Song for No Words," Vol. XII, No. 3, Autumn, 1959;

"Invitation to a Hay," Vol. XII, No. 3, Autumn, 1959; " 'Thy Love Is One Thou'st Not Yet Known,' " Vol. XV, No. 4, Winter, 1962–1963; "Pays Perdu," Vol. XVII, No. 3, Autumn, 1964. "Morality" and "Beside a Fall" were first published in *The New York Times*.

Many of these poems were written on a Guggenheim Fellowship, an honor and aid of which the author is deeply sensible.

For My Mother

Contents

❧ ONE ☙

❧ TWO ☙

❧ THREE ❧

❧ FOUR ❧

x

❧ FIVE ❦

ONE

Cortège for Colette (THE PALAIS-ROYAL GARDENS)

Minister of birds, islands and pools,
Familiar of shade by the hushed walk of sedges,
Collector of grasses, seed-heavy and bent,
Who gather the violet seed and the grape
(known to the moonmen and the green fever),
All receipts and brews, felicitous cures
Under sinewy roofs and streets of the root . . .

Genius, moreover, of gardens,
The bowknot, the crescent, and square,
And as many circular knots, and that pruning art
The shears do so well with the snail,
Tender and trainer of fountains,
Benefactor of box, quincunx, and yew,
Mathematician of the parterres
By a lapful of sparrows,

I have heard, I have come by these arches and urns,
All the classical battery of forms
Through the rectangular perspectives
Down the long galleries that end in the windows.
Closed are the gates. The calm is great
In the dark, where the small waters blow.
There is a sense of a slow sailing out
As a sudden wind tries a few leaves.
A part of a cloud interrupts the passage
Of the knobbed moon.

And I do not think the garden is what it was.
Like a promise departed, the rectangular perspectives
Down the long galleries end in the windows,
Stop with the shutters.
Should I speak I would not be heard
There where the moon slowly sails on,
For where might there be another speech
Such as signs give, and omens,

3

Such as sense has in those dreams
For which there is no translation except
In the absolutely unheard music about, perhaps, to be given,
Like a part of the secret sky broken off
Just at the surface where it crowds
With those vaguely summoned to take the long turns of the dance?

But let me not, standing outside these gardens,
These oblong gardens, behind the closed gates,
Where only some sliver of water sighs,
Spilling over and over into its pool,
Where under the yellow light of the lamps
Only a cat walks, it is late for the arcades
Out of the gardens to keep their own life,
And for low doors opening into mossed courts,
Let me not, to the diminished perspectives
Hovered with ivy where an urn sits,
                                        declare
That a part of the world having gone back into itself,
A meaning is thereby lost,
The disappearance of which torments us,
For it was not subtle but gross.

Amidst all this matching of flowers and shapes,
This tending of borders, this cutting by trowels,
Though compelled to pay close attention and not to walk blindly
As if in a massacre of petals,

To know
That that of which you were the great witness lives,
That the torn butterfly will not leave the page,
Pierced by the light you gave,
That by the power not to forget
Profoundly connecting with the root
You brought by its weight some perfected whole
Of a part of the self into flower,
Who lightly go to the grave,
Having expended all you could give.

Nor to speak of the corruption of ivy
Nor of absence where presence dwells

4

Nor of darkness where there is love.
To be mute, to be mute about death,
To address the invisibles
For whom your genius, like a delicate beast
Training your heart,
To your sense giving lessons,
Led you out of the one world
Into how many nuages—portents, embarkings!

And simply to lift up the flower,
Simply to salute the cloud,
From the cat to the horse by way of the dragon,
To some striped sky by way of the bird

That it be borne, your body,
In the arms of young men round and round
And to the march blown by bugles
That the dark iron of its velvet vow
Shock through the blood some understanding
Just as surpassing as when the touched body
Gives forth the divine humors of rain, leaves, and love.

Amsterdam Letter

Brick distinguishes this country,
And broad windows—rather, rectangles
Of wide and glittering scope—
And cabbages.
Cattle a specialty, and cheese, storks—if they are not all dead
Or abandoned—and flowers, oh, flowers!
Some say as well, quick humor.
Is it a specimen of humor that a cabdriver proposes to marry me?
The speaking of English is at least general.
I have spoken as well a little Dutch with an old Frisian lady.
How affable she was, amusing and helpful!
(They *are* helpful and affable, and their far too occasional teams of
horses
Wear rosettes by the ears.)
Aside from that, and above all, the dense, heavy, fragrant sky
And rich water, a further extension of color—
The sky a low window over this twining of green water and bridges—
And the sedate, gabled houses pressed closely together
And bicyclists, six abreast or more,
Skimming round corners like swallows.
How quiet they are! Even the trolleys!
While the trains seem to glide like sleighs on runners
So that after those many places dedicated, it would seem, to clatter,
The absence of it becomes an active delight in itself.

The delight is in part, of course, the lovely dividing of the city
By those ancient and ripe-green canals, and the mixed fragrance
Of the River Amstel and roasting coffee,
And the bravura of carved animal heads, the elegance of panels,
And those panes of violet and panes flushed yellow
(To transmit the effect of sunlight in winter?)
That alternate the pure meaning of glass
With the blindness of shutters closed over warehouse windows,
And that Gothic German-French sense of the arabesque and the
scroll,
The urn and the garland of leaves.

6

As for that delicacy of manner, that responsiveness to many,
That prevalence of what seems self-possessed, contained, and easy—
I am speaking of those who went out of their way
To lead me to Rembrandt's house
(Which in his lifetime he lost),
Of the woman at the Cantine,
Of the Madame, too, in the Zeedijk,
Amiable conversationalists
Who did not make me feel stupid
Because I would never speak their language,
Who by a manner suggested
What I have no word for—
Unfeigned it is and unblighted,
That "generous, free disposition"
That so strongly confirms
A fitness of things,
As do also the upright geraniums,
All of which, by the elm-dark canals
(Where dogs on the loose loped up to me
With cold, wet noses
And ducks paddled under the Seven Arches
And the gilt swan rode on the crest of the fortified tower),
Offered some measurable glimpse of what
There, by the water beds
And the ancient, calmed passions of their reflections,
Informed me as the moon does,
Which was in part the pleasure of learning
Those words that I did from the old Frisian woman—
Horse, sky, cow, tree, thank you, I mean,
Beauty, and love.

Invitation to a Hay

A settlement of love
Is what I'd risk if you would.
A central fountain and a horse,
A little native elegance,
Some green-shuttered saffron buildings,
Avenues of leaning trees
And an orchard close by
Divided from a field of hay
By a moldering old wall
Snaking up a hill.
I'd have a garden primed
With beanflowers and chick-peas
And in tubs lemon trees
Not to forget the marveled orange—
Where is a fruit so bright
And a stem so delicate?—
And days of blue air
That crowd the dark boughs of a grove
And other days as pale
As wind in a birch grove—
Oh, birch, my very white
And airy delight!
And back of us and all around
For the castle-haunting rooks
To fly to and fro from
The many-sided, dark blue-faced
Mountains, wrinkled, ravined, cleft
When they are not cast upon
By those pallors that beyond
Tell of a snowlight's origin.
And in this civil order
Ringed round by a wilderness
I'd have some very conical
And shaggy house of hay

To invite you in to stay
As long as butter-yellow walls pleased you.
And there you'd be with me,
We'd live in a monument of hay
Mad as those who know
In love is all fantasy.
Your breast would be of burning gold
And its delicious heat
Would warm me day and night
While creatures of the wood
Might envy, if they could,
Our joy just as fine
As the improvising clouds
That as you look at them are gone,
Or volatile as leaves in wind
Flying forth from us,
Not to be contained.
We'd go bird-nesting in clouds
And hunting down the meadow grass
For flowers or the smallest haunts
Of the young field mice.
And in this ancient landscape
Preponderant with moss,
Rambling walls and pinewoods
Of narrow alleys at the end of which
Daylight stares starkly through,
Our love alone would be new
Despite its ancient properties.
Ariel would we be
With love's finest courtesies,
By all that shapes of earth and air
Can subtilize the senses with
Until they have grown rapt
On emanations of a light
When fold on fold goes into
Five fathoms of a blue.
Our love would be endowed
By mountain and by cloud
So long as we would stay

Alongside such ravines
And such slopes of terraced vines
Broken towers and bells
In a shaggy house of hay.
My dear, and will you be
Content to dwell with me
Eating of illusion
Daily and nightly?

Of a Day and Hares

Dürer's brown hares were in a cage
With their long soft ears laid flat,
Their oblong eyes closed, in some feigned sleep,
Only their whiskers alive
In the perpetual tremor of very fine things.
A guinea pig to each hare slept on each hare's back.
It was, for September, a hot day
And there was that fur close to fur and warming it.

We have lost much time by love affairs,
By a pedantic madness we have lost the rest.
Animals have time. We lose it.
When we lose we are lost. We are marking time with the days,
We are letting them die away.
In retrospect we see the dwindling host,
We are fierce judges of what costs us tears most.
To judge ourselves is as to see ourselves
Grandiose in plight. We see ourselves and think that we may laugh.
Salubrious is laughter. Or a short barking unhappy and ugly.
If we would not lose time, what would we be?
That which no doubt we are.
But does it alter? Perhaps.
If between being and doing there were not a gulf.
The animals for whom we have too much respect of a sentimental
Variety
Supposedly dwell in the mindless flow. Is being mindless purity?
Does it partake of an indefinable grace?
We lie down in the grass and hear time moving over us.
Its bells that flay the air flay us.
Or in the light rumble of its wheels the weight is going over us.

Or then to stroll . . .
Alone before God or nothingness. . . .
For the guinea pigs and the hares will be sold
Or caged. Only the air we cannot use
Or hurt is free. Only the air and light we cannot cage
That play upon this day so soundlessly. . . .

Remember That Country

My dear, do you remember that country
Of abandoned stone houses with their roofs toppled in,
Eyes of their windows blank sockets,
Great nest-holes for birds and ways for the wind?
Steps to them crumbling, the grasses grown wild,
Half hay and half weed in the gardens?
And the ascensions and erosions of mountains
Sharply arising from the river's deep basin
Where the hilltowns sat in their jagged nests,
Abandoned as well, and dying.
Ancient, so ancient, built
In the times of the Saracens
When the only defense was retreat
And triple-made bastions of walls out of rock,
So old, who had been driven so far
Up to such verges, to live at all.
Do you remember, and the deep gorges,
Those long gashes in earth the river had cut,
Very fantasias of concentric circles of rock
Up which the stream's bed went?
And the joy of the day, the way the birds sang,
The sun on the river, the rosemary and lavender,
Do you remember the fête and the danceband
To which the nightingales sang?
And the women washing clothes
In the brimmed stone tubs on the turns of the way
Up to the first of those towns so crookedly set
On crazy needles of rock?
And the goat bleating in a shut-in stable?
Do you remember? It was you set the pace,
You would take every zigzag path, .
Given up to the vigils of knowing and seeking,
Intolerably wanting to touch every crest,
Go back of each mountain into the stilled

Frozen seas of their wilderness.
That day when we were parched with thirst
It was you who discovered the medlar.
How we robbed that tree of its fruit
For the taste of its happiness!
Do you remember? Such distances!
Such echoes! So many towers!
And the great river we walked by
So many miles! All that had happened!
Such thickness of leaves should you turn to the legends,
The Sieges, the Plague, the Wars of Religion,
The countships, the courts of love
And the olives and lizards by the clamorous river
Drowning our voices as it drowned theirs
That had their eyes once and their bodies,
Stones that they threw, songs that they sang,
And their kisses.
Do you remember those discarded old bridges
Still sustaining substantially
Spans for mere marguerites to take,
In such slow travel, along with the poppies,
Where wagons and horsemen once went?
And that army of sheep back from some grassland,
And their heat, so close-pressed, though they
Were new-shaven, the tremolo of their baas
And their dogs, the donkeys, and shepherds?
Then there was that yellow wild flower
Casting up such fresh gusts of fragrance
That it, broken by the night-singing of birds,
Shall sum up for the rest of my days
An unsullied country, almost beyond the stars.

"Thy Love Is One Thou'st Not Yet Known"

Let us be quiet today. The earth is still,
The sun is drowsy, sleeping in the clouds
Like sleepless birds of day who take to rest
Or take at least to silence in their nests
Only some very few adventured out
To stride the levels of the rusty grass.

But for the crickets in a singsong shrill
Of notes too small to be called notes,
Some tick and jilt of quaver in the low tangle
Soprano as some fifing of an elf
Or other hopping creatures made of green,
Green-whiskered, green-antennaed, green-armored,
There is no other cry or breath.
                      Air is still
As every flower tells and every leaf,
And waters where they were subside to wells
Or sink their resourceful chatter underground.

As if the quick of all that stir and bloom
By brook and wind commotion, ceaseless play
Of clouds, leaves, action of the plants
That in their beds stand taller every day
Had taken a quietus or, quiescent,
Retired into some first most voiceless place
Begot by silence on a stillness,
An in-going into the unlustred zone
Of some more hermit energy
That gets the tendrils of the sense
Their dwelling place in a white hush

And makes the instant finer than a dream.
But is not dream but rather's known
By burning fineness of a light
More lucid than the air and only sensed
In violent wide-awakeness on a cloud.

Only by the raveling of such bonds
As strips the day to garments of the flower—
To leaning lilies much too tall
To sustain their flaring crowns,
Veronica, vervain, bent over by the rain,
And Queen Anne's lace upon its gawky stem.

Words with an Orchard Tree

You boughs hung here with flower
By what strain may I trace
In wind, water, and air,

By what line lithe as vine
May I there ascend,
Young tree of no fruit

But this pale bloom you bear,
To your effect of flower
Tranced in a bower?

"By paint or pen that limns
Myself so well I stand
As if in sun and wind

That will not warp nor wear,
By song that may shape
In air that I live on

An unwithering garland.
What else may translate
My drifts of rose and white,

My boughs grown very wand
Of the crimson bud?"
Young tree, I too would sing

Of the flower that grows
Meshed in the mists of mind.
It is the allegorical thing,

It is the single sheaf that binds
Flower and what's dreamed upon
By the flower of its pure form.

Variations

This was a day so strange,
A changeling day, it was
Like none other that had been
Or might come again.
The silence, first, that was
So porous, moist and cool
(Like air the rain has fallen through)
It closed its muteness like a wall
Round twenty fields of air
And was a substanced thing of hush
In a contracted sphere.
The birds, next, who from
The first moment of dawn
Set out to sing all day.
Not one moment that was not
Linked to the next
By notes so caught with other notes
It seemed a net got wove
Through which the music could not pass
But was retained
Or perpetuated in refrain
The inundating silvers, one by one.
It was a day for every bird
To be in his best tune.
The flowers, next. The day had
As many flowers as birds.
The middle of the May brought
Her orchard and her lilac.
A half of grass was deeply drowned
By the violet.
And silence. Foremost of cloud
Or of air strung through
With those broken vapors of
Invisible cloud bloom.

Foremost the flowers then.
Their sheathes and rooty feet
Gave air a body cloud could not
To make it mute and resonant.
Subtending a resilient stillness
That each note might prevail,
They from their fibrous dens
Listened in a drowse of pearl
And what applause they gave was myrrh.
Such gifts urged more tests
Of birds to see who sang best,
The day was an Eden's year.

On the Legends of a Dancer

I was a child in a small midwestern town,
It was a still summer afternoon
Yellow under the great maple trees.
Perfumes of the close-shorn grass and the entranced
Loose-hanging clusters of dark-laced boughs
Sealed me into the heat of a grape-enclosed
Urn of summer's drowse
Under the arbors of vine-weaving ease
When a beautiful woman, my mother's friend,
Famed for her girlhood of violets and beau-taking
Sashes, valances at dances, of supreme
Dew-drenched, liquid-kissing, cyclamen-haunted eyes,
Came to inform us that you were dead.
Into which with the speaking of faraway *death* was mixed
A coquettish condemnation of ardors so fierce
It seemed leopards might spring from the dots and cirques
Of a heat-ringed shade stippled by sun on the wands of the boughs.
And a vast sadness commingled with a vast sense
Of a mystery so obscurely profound
Seemed to wring from the antiphonies
Of an everywhere that the trees described
A music flowing up from their roots
And down through the whole shivering sap of their lives
Whereupon it seemed that I understood
Love, womanhood, and dancing.

Eulogy and Elegy

Farewells and leavings! Ships fanning the waters
And so many thousands of handkerchiefs—sails
Winging up to clouds, gulls languorously
Keeling these glades, whistles and rumors,
Bells! And our hearts anchored till it'd seem
We'd go with the ropes, *Leerdam,* and tear
With these volumes, throats from which
All staples mount the very forehead of prows!
She beats from her moorings and quietly glides,
Leaning, into the river. Past the black
Battled shorelines of rails, towers,
And so with the ease of eyes
Glides and slides down to the evening.
Then come the rims and the rings,
Plateaus and prairies till the whole steep
Of the horizon nears
And it is all sea! sea! sky-shouldering roof-
Combs of the fanged thousand mouths.
Angels! And were you not prepared
For the warmths and the startings—
We were uprooted from rocks by the clanging,
The ship sprang at us and on our breasts
Bore there, intaglio'd weeping.
Forests of pierwood, copper of stations,
Humps of the islands, lost portals!
Did you not know our beginnings?
Oh, then by the buoys' pastured cries tossed, tossing,
To come at last into the gangways of morning!
Sight that leaps with the freshness of stars!
Ancient palladiums! Gong for all goings!

TWO

For the Circuit of the Orpheum and the Isis

Where are the stars of our rich balconies
When roosted with the pigeons we would stare
In hopeless schoolgirl fashion at some dark
Small dapper and silk-suited god
Chanting in a spotlight all our loves
And playing with delicious frippery
Upon our harp-strung nerves to see him so
And thus to see him so to think his gaze
Beneath the fixed white lightning tranced
Had trained, transfixed, upon our own
What we as much caught up in it returned:

And those white doves that the magician feigned
Forth by such an elegance to come
From out a long and silken handkerchief?
Dexterity, the pleasure of the sense,
Raised to some most lissome, slipping height,
And all commanded at a dreamlike pace:
The birds, the cards he glides into his hat,
The birds that sit on perches in their cage
Once he has made them out of air
And that long flow of undulating scarf:

And where the loose and practiced acrobats,
The frantic clowns ablaze with lunacy
And pistol shots and waterworks and firecrackers
That light the coda of a second tale,
Saints of our tired mortality who get
The kick-in-the-pants with punctual artlessness
As being that which lunacy desires:

And where, and where the old guards of the hall,
Each with his act that lasts a briefest while,
Simple, irrelevant, and based
On what they figure will connect us all:
Gauche and *louche* and rude and wet

And fake with hot sweet tears that soon dry up,
And where lost innocence and all its troupe
Put up in paper sunsets for the sale?

O blue-eyed lie, you know it's true,
Some sums of living are we would forget
All that we never wished to know.
If this is the wisdom of the booby trap
Then let these pranksters deal it like
Pages from the gull's hornbook
To that soft vertigo the violin's mew starts up

The while we come to laugh our anger out
And laugh here in the demi-dark,
The sands of charm now heavy in our eyes
At this mock world that plays at ducks and drakes
With all our devil worship for what hurts
And all our heavy reverence for the real—
Like some exact machinery blowing up.

It is a trick: it tells us just as much
As that bright horse who does arithmetic.
But then—the pratfalls and the miracles
And one low voice that cries it lives
And one low voice that cries it lives
And one low voice that cries it lives by love.

New York: Summertime

Those rumors and orchestras
Of the playgrounds of summer—
Children!
Parked trucks of the ovaled cheeks
And sleek skin of the cut watermelon!
Bells of the traveling parlors
And snow-wagons of ice cream!

Your pale stifling room
Glazed by the porcelain light
Of pulled Venetian slats.
Half-naked now we sit
Our arms so bare we seem to touch
Though we don't do so
And so much else exposed
Through your walkup's open doors—
The husband in his underwear,
The sweating housewife slumped
On a kitchen chair,
Van Gogh prints and mottoes on the walls—
"Here is the time to live and why not now!"

In your room's glazed pallor
The oven's burning toast.
Your many mirrors garble
Parts of light and float.
Touch is burning up the toast,
The mirrors scorch that hold
Our drowned-in-shadow faces in them.
Boop of the saxophone.
Those sugar'd waltzes slurping.
It is! I am! I am! screams
Summer in a heat.
It is! You are! You are!
My stupored blood beats back.

25

And you, child of the violent season,
Who buy your playtime in the bars,
Who'd blaze away the moment like they do
Upon their hopscotch squares
Or by some streetlamp shrilling late
With cards and fires—
They tell me how your nature's blent
With what's so shaped and colored still
By this half-cracked omphalos of
The fevers of our screwed-up fate—
O crazes of the dynamo!

Your restless energy that thirsts!
Your forced elations that like rockets burst
Their salvos upon nothingness!
A spendthrift tempest that I hear
Your hammering heart beat out
To the convulsive pulse
Our motored generations make!

2

And you, child of the violent season,
The summer's kissing you.
A *blague*. It's I who kiss
It's I who strive in blood
To get this mixing done
Of motored air that whines
With the continuous burr
Of exiled insects dead.
Some desiccated grief-in-fear
Now in the populous midst
Of energies that strain
With passion at the leash
Because it is the time to live!
Because exploding chemistries
Tell us so and tell
Of the hurled-at star. (We hear
The howling dog in space.)
Our fate like his is brief and short,

Succinct as melting summer on the limbs
Though in the senseless go
Of bodies to get wet and faint
We may feel less isolate.

Now, put up in quietude,
Freed of that frenzied churn,
It's you and you and you who still beat on
To make the wild percussion in my mind
Though it's the mourning dove that moans
And deafening crickets grind
Against those pastimes of the horn
The sizzling locusts wind
And tattered hollyhocks decline.

That bounding ball, the radios
That played around your court,
Your frittered pulse that leapt
With the stertorous breath
That twists an impulse into flame—
Of these I make my monody:
To action that pretends it knows,
To necessity that says
It was before we chose
What we're burning in,
To our splendor and our waste.

Out of the Cynic's Chapbook

All affection and all love
Come to this when god is done
(And they killed the unicorn),
That memory is unpunctual and we must
Make money first before we dare
To give the kiss and hand.
Next, be cheerful, apt, alert
At seizing every chance to get
Unnamable goals that mark us the elect.

All affection and all love
Prove next: choose what succeeds,
Learn skills by which to distinguish sheep,
The dashing from the fathomable
And shameful slack-wills from the steel-geared ones.
And he who languors in the cistern dark
Commutes his question to those insolent powers,
The skies and clouds, that tell him not
And whose escaping grandeur galls
The petty end for which he lives and hurts.

Then think not twice—complain never.
Be brushed and scrubbed, live—like the automobile!
And useful then, speed others to their goal
Fleeing from their furies one more mile.

But heart, it is this cynic pang
Whose numbing poison would deliver you
For all your protest to the thing you hate,
For when you saw them ride the flowered boughs down
You doubted more the flowers than those who rode
And you have mocked with love turned back upon itself
Those wide precarious prospects, dream-enlarged,
That this mechanic show would have you pawn:
Your dream for its; that's part of it,
Although it means no harm:

It simply wants its way, which means your life.
And yet it has its sentiments like everyone.
Speak to it softly, it will answer you
Anent the "higher things that all men strive for"
The while it'd have you call your angels clowns
And with swarmed wisdom denigrate
All that you'd lived for once.
Do this: they'll hail you as their very own
Before, laughing, they thrust you down and down.

New England Town

Of the Horseshow Tavern, Frenchy's cat
With the whiteface that I saw
Crawl through a broken basement window
And come out, as black as coal,
Of Duke's, the red American Legion Hall,
And that toplofty wooden ark
With Swiss-Italian gables and broad eaves
That built onto, extends a nest of rooms
For gay yards back and three alleys,
I speak, and of those pallid little towns
Where thread is wound, and spindles whirr
With that malicious tension of machines.
You find them in the low hills of blue dew
Or jungled in the sunset thickets, caught
Where light resplendent tosses off from crosses
A tarnished beam down trees.
And they are huddled, poor, and mean
Strung out without a center, of no shape
Except as emptiness can make,
And you are haunted by the way
A meagre dullness seems to say
This is the Real and this is all of it.
Until at five the dark pours in
Let down from hills on violet trays,
Tiers of the smoky stuff through which
The white bone of a steeple juts.
An end to plainness double-crossed
And grubby modesty that came to terms
With this squashed thing it has to call a life!
You wish it were. You turn to go.
Too much this marvelous promise of the mist
Would make you think the clear was not the true.
It is such stealth as this embalms the soul.

A Note to La Fontaine

I have come into the time of the ant.
The grasshoppers are bitterly paying.
Their fiddles are broken, they are lame and laid up,
The ants are sneering: "Now dance!"
And the grasshoppers, in an ague of shivering,
Faint for a morsel, seem to be trying.
It is not good to see. How may I have my tribe starve?
It is a slap in the face of all I believe
To concede that the sour ones, safe in their barracks
Where they so promiscuously scurry,
Should have every right to be dry and ironic.
Survival is *not* the test, and is a long life the best?
Fie on the envious dullards
Who brag of their sweltering summer labor
That they may live without honor through winter.
The grasshoppers have more grace
Than to make out for themselves any case.
With that knowledge they'll die
Spitting into the bleak eye
Of those who never had such song
To make life seem beautiful and warm.

Epitaph for My Cat

And now my pampered beast
Who hated to be wet,
The rain falls all night
And you are under it.
Who liked to be warm,
Are cold as any stone,
Who kept so clean and neat,
Cast down in the dirt
Of death's filthy sport.

Jazz Bit

Go lift that pane of moonlight from the floor
And tell Nicotiana to stop
Screaming with her perfume.
The Four o'Clocks too. They're drunk with dew.

I gotta date with a hoot owl,
I gotta date with a whoo.
Wait for the bird. By the moon-soaked wall,
By the insect's hairy legs.
Wait for that green funeral
Of the cricket in a pall.
Wait for the knell that tolls a moth,
A vast robin as well,
Who died last week
Of the invisible wound that kills a crow.
Wait till the master of all vermin,
Presiding genius of the graves,
Comes with his rats, mice, frogs, toads, and bugs.
"Light, I salute thee but with wounded nerves!"

Of the Incas

By what malignancy of secret orders
Came the horse-foamed doom,
The cocks whose hoarse halloos said *blood*
And *blood* again with trumpeting?

They had not couched the vainglory of that question.
They'd read the stars for other potencies
And out of terror civilization made
An order of the harvests. To the dead
Were given gauntlets and gold masks
To wear upon their mummying.

Before the Thing that came there had been signs:
Division of the kingdom had begun;
A rumor, too, by earlier kings
That masters of the lightning would descend;
The earth trembling, a condor set upon,
That horror sacred to the gods brought down;
Such portents to the currents of their blood
Reversed its action till the immensity
Of what they thought must be loomed great in them.

And when the invader came with weights and wheels
Forth from his councils with the hard Unknown
To get his gold and drive time's battering rams
Convulsive with the cross at their carved stones
On which a jaguared wrath had once been dug,
It was the surge of what they had foreknown,
The omen bodied forth they reeling met
And reeling sank before. It had been seen,
What issued from the center of the world.

The while the gold was melted and a thousand years
Fell with the dust of temples and there ran
The Conquest's course before it plunged
To the crevasses that had once been spanned.

They Guided Birds (THE CONQUEST OF PERU)

They guided birds and came to hear their story
At that astounding hour famous to birds
When mirthful on light's nourishment they go
Wild with tournaments of cries upon the air—
At wing feats are as angels, light as flowers
That glide and skate the upbeats and whirl down
With that velocity that only air allows
And dreaded most the still hour when all went
Cut of a sudden by some quick response
To that which flares no longer bird blood up.

They guided birds and were at one with birds,
At one with lizards gloating in the sun
Feverish and dry, their little throats swollen,
Nor had time bells nor wheels nor did they count
Sands that ran through the glass relentlessly,
It simply set the sun and swung with seas,
In the rare mountains it was not at all
Nor had the self a shadow save of wings.

And was their life an abundance as of birds,
Had they for blood a bird-blood sad and gay?
We do not know; what questions caged
Birds in their thickets till they sang no more?
The wiry air was free with its whole light,
The sun a potency they understood
And by it got great harvests and as well
From earth a curious sun-like thing
From which they made gold gardens for their One,
And disks to mirror the round sun's ruddy head,
And light was in this instance fixed and firm.

And time was as the shadows of the birds
Declining and arising in their play.
In time they learned by study of the stars
To read of those first waters of immensity

By which unfevered stars arose, and birds,
And patient seeds they set flowered into grain.
The birds were masters of transparency
And they were heavy with a thing not born.

Until those enemies and foes of birds
Self-seeking, ravening, and mad for gold,
Thrust through the thickets of the long blue days.
Then all fell down; the birds in headlong droves,
The realm divided, taken prisoner,
The gold brought in to fill a room or more
To please another One back home.
Bird-self sent underground, bird-blood
In harness, bird-blood taxed
To pay an invalid thing, and stillness came,
The thing they'd learned to dread, and reigned.

Proem

Now waiting in difficult rooms of justice
For the assent that will not come, insurrecting theorem
On which could have been based the dissident structure of happiness:

And waiting in the brown dispassionate autumn
Grimacing with rain as leaves are mashed
By the hard errands of the anonymous foot

Under the monotonous sky that governs plains
And ruins, declensions of the past's soiled promissory,
Counting the time until the full hour blows

Among the leaves and fall of hours
When voices rash with envy, retribution
Mouth once again the well-bred lies

Of neat and heavy houses where
Regularity would stifle difference, rebellion
Is an adolescent vice, typical of the spoiled, ungifted derelict:

I would search out the subject that will not decay,
Willing that by such patience I will not lose patience
Despite the inchworm crawl of this destructive time,

Crude refuse, backwash of the late disfigured past,
Nor bay against the dogs of dissolution.
So if crude action tells again my deaths

And wounds are quicked to life: the gape begins
Impossible to stanch, a kind of inorganic struggle of the blood:
Yet by resolve build resource, set

Faith at insult, love against the crazed impulse
To hate, and so find calm in terror.
The wet leaves molder, pale, and turn to meal

And waiting's less a test of revelation
Than test to see how quietly I turn
And cur-like snarl at what I'd once cherished

When back like scavengers my gifts return
Loathed, now loathsome, that were once so hearty.
And thus, like one before the dead

Paused so and huddled like a thick bundle,
To stand against these broken meanings that would paralyze
And sting to death the separate parts of consciousness

Or conscience, in an inactive hell.
And wait: as if a continuity
Inheres, outweighs, like roots, this passageway of leaves

So harshly driven to yield up their place:
Knowing full well how once again such waiting may be dupe,
Fiasco occasioned by the overt lack,

Arraigned as well by gorged and slippery luck.
More useless than a broken arm the gun
Or all defense against the terrible one,

Or all offense, old leader love.
Dead angel we deceive. . . .

THREE

Last Letter to the Scholar

Come, lecturer on love, resume your rostrum.
Preach to the mad dead roses of the year.
Preach to my heart that's buried in the garden
Under the yellowed petals since you left.
Though deaf by those haranguing winds
The winter plagues dead petals with, and leaves
Long fluttering upon the barren ground or straying
Around the broken stems and shackled thorns,
Your voice by its compelling sweetness will
Spring to winter bring, and numb roots start
Alive to pierce and quick the dark
That closed around with killing cold what heart
I had, after you'd come and left.

My dear, you'll call this fallacy
Pretentious, or some fustian idiocy
To claim my ticking heart was put from me
Into some troped-up garden of old rue.
Forgive, because I set up roses too,
Improbable as madrigals. And chide
My errant language that would claim
I died, or nearly died, for loss of you.
Chide, but believe. I live, but I am dead.
But that's not what I mean. Who lives
Must learn to live his deaths. Who loves
Must learn the same. We blaze and char
As love is near or far
In that small world that's ordered to our want
But likewise bounded by love's eyes and lips.
The expanded world thus so contracted, what
Fires that come consume us when they're out.
And death's more amorous than not
And just as subtle sudden and chameleon cruel.

So preach to me, and tell me less of death
Than love that outlasts death, as I've heard tell.

41

Tell me that my heart confined
And sunken low within the flesh's earth
Will, when you come again, awake
And know its Easter in your sight
As may those thwarted roses rise
Some later on to your rare light
Compounded of much heat and spirit.
Tell me that this death's not long.
Be hortatory, admonitory, and calm
In your bright fever, that the clear estate
The world is when you're here will get again
Its lease to be, as you propound
How to our destiny we grow as one
If two, with such split hearts as we own,
Not sanguined by experience, may so dream
An absolution clement as the rain.

Sleep was all that speech

Sleep was all that speech my heart choked up.
I lingered there in cobbled squares of dew
Until the bird before the window woke and supped.
A bell sent others clambering and I shook.

And what if the all-but human is just this
Power at the mighty peephole of the sun?
Or those convivial horns that chime and split?
Fabulous eyes. How you'll be buried there.

Or then—the rose awning over the day—
To be strung by every bone and pinioned there—
What if the motor broke, the purpose run,
Twist, torment, dance and hang be done?

The truth connects us but the more is love—
Without that top to wind, no way to go
Celebrants all, of the ladder up the mow
And children calling—smoke forms of the snow!

Small Song

Take back that look. Close the door
To that shuttered room.
The thought of what we left, forget.
Those shadows, too, that let
Such thirst for what we said not, in.

Those beads of memory you tell,
Tell no more. Their perfume still,
The subtle drug and wine.
Cover you. Put glasses on.
Feign, conceal, lest we begin

What well we know must end. So, so,
No last lamenting kiss, but go!

Rose. . . . .

Rose, I have spent three days
Having nothing better to do
In an extremely useful society
Than to gaze at you.
The poem cannot exceed us
Nor my nature, your art.

Oh, but don't pull the spines out!
You are so flagrant and still
There must be a dark blood somewhere
From the severe disorder you make
Or there might be a way to embalm me in you
Delusions thus make desperate.

I dreamed of a cage for such flowers
That butterflies despaired of.
I dreamed of the terror pressed
Against the heart by your dark leafy dress
And the enforced violence, the scraping
Of blood in the chest by this.

But don't listen to me.
I only just whisper to you.

What Tender Bough

What day has come? What sudden world is here?
Leaves overnight spend out their green surprise
And that seditious lord of brine and tear
Is felled awhile by cloudy enterprise.

Now hoops and jigs inebriate the child!
As princes hunt their tigers down a sward
He drives his birds before him on the mall.
What air is this? What tender bough?

Invasion of the blood by lilac oil!
While in the ports of touch and taste
New fumes and ichors detonate.
We lie all gentled by the wounds of joy.

Is green the color of the soul? Snow-white
In snow, the world is brined with salt,
Its wounds the mind's wound and its thought
In winter's salt kept dark, by darkness pent.

Red-wined beneath the leaves' whirled canopies
The world is green or red where it was white
With darkness that the white cleansed not.
Now it is green. We marvel at such light.

Delirious impulse, tigers, child,
Send forth your joy against that stricken night
When he of taloned faculties awakes.
Long is his proof. Let joy be bright.

Strong is his power by which he binds
His weighty proof with thew and thong.
Let joy be sinewed at his iron bands,
Joy be not rent but he by joy's quick hands.

Let joy be long, be long.

How I Loved

How I loved that one of the dark gaze
More sombre than velvet and fire.
So were you, my trepidation of touch
To the tear's deep draught when I dreamt.
We are mad to seek in the Low Countries
For that which comes once. Watch when it comes!
May you watch for the star that the day enslaves?
Remember thereafter! in the pent skies
How suddenly untrammeled it flushed into light—
Shy blaze of its pain bearing forth such rays
In the far gardens the evening prepares—
Of whose vows that our tryst pledged in the cup
The birds, going forth, sang as they burned
Steeped in those dyes, even as we,
Terrifying under high ceilings of snow. . . .

The Adam Tree

We know it for the way it drags us back
The whole long length of years, that Dying House
Of Familied Life, the doting kin come round
To sit and claw at fading Papa's name,
Judge and captain of the mannered crew.
The longueurs of the tribal jokes and dogs
The aunts and cousins at some third remove
Come miles to mourn the pillar tottering down
And suffer every baked meat of the clan
The duteous Bible-keepers of the deeds—
For every petted pride a dividend
That kept the stranger out and sweet kith in
And with the belief in family, belief in God
And the unwithering state, great three-in-one—
Those tintype faces of remote small boys,
Hues of ancestral skies in every gaze!
And know it for the stifling in their bosoms,
The dark that would not thaw, the smothering down
When punctually they gather round the board
Where grandma's lain in bonds, her taint passed on.
No victory from her aims—how fallen, fallen!—
The wheel is set. Although they rage to go
Into the soft cold madness of the snow
Or anywhere! beyond the blooded brags!
To smash, if nothing else, the vase from China
Inspect the high-born motives of some Uncle,
Know Mother for what she did not want to do
And Death the testy teacher of them all . . .

I thought that when I heard your praise
Curse your ancestral myths, hegemonies
That hounded more than them down in the grave
And changed sunk eyes for stars.
The old dead froze you more than I
After you lied and made a dupe of hope

And in their grip you toiled the august way
That stifles tongues and hardens every mask
Resourceful men hang up to trade upon
When Furies hiss from far off down the road.
Your holdings sold, your woods and groves long cut,
And you still climbing up the crooked tree
To tie dry leaves and withered fruits back on.
You scared off birds and porcupines by this.
How can an old man climb so agilely?
No springs have come I ever liked as much
After the day you sneered and I played jade
To the rich you got because it paid to charm
After those boughs snapped in the sundering shade.

Night glitters and the rash return

Night glitters and the rash return of those
Dissentient winds the pale spring has
And earnest hillsides sporting with their bulbs
Convince me, with the moon, the new time buds
Though dark my body and ill-kempt
From some lopped want whose anguish is a hate.
The winds bang late. A gale that wrests those tendrils
From their stems now flings at me; dust claps
And rolls against my mouth like ill-said lies
Disgorged with staling vehemence from dull skies
Where lovers' truths have blotted out the day.
My hunger leaps and dies. What lovers' truths
Aren't like a parody; most honest lies,
The imprecisions of a proud disease.
The moon goes up the sky and I am knived
By that distrust that breeds itself anew
From every absence that we jailors seize.
I bed you with all whores, two-headed wives,
Conjure your instant perfidies and crook
Their mongrel upstarts in my arms.
What monsters I beget now turn on me
To rend this worst of all, my tiger want
To paint your portrait with my heart's harsh black.

The chill crisp daffodils who've just come out
Have nothing left to do.
And are these hillsides sprouting with mere dew?
An oblong gesture from the moon's horns hurt
That less than moony lustre of the night.
May round winds bring my words all back
A later instant from their starting out
And gag me with their judas-mimic crew.

Upon the Intimation of Love's Mortality

It is the effort of the lie
Exacts a wounding pulse.
I loved you much
When everything had excellence at once.
First was our freshness and the stun of that.
Your body raved with music. What was lost
Is just that element our time always takes
And always in love we venture off some height
That nothing else can equal after it.
The thought of that bedevils me for miles.
How can I save you from my own despair
To think I may not love you as before?
Spoiled, we become accustomed to our luck.
This is the devil of the heart.
We were the smiles of gods awhile
And now, it seems, our ghosts must eat us up
Or wail in temples till our tombs are bought.
Attended now by shades of that great while,
Disguise is the nature of my guile
And yet the lie benumbs the soul.
Get me the purity of first sight!
Or strength to bear the truth of after light!

"When shall we set sail for happiness?"
—BAUDELAIRE

Darling, I dreamed alone without you
In our bed disordered and stained by wine
That delirious for ships we went down to ports
And swathed in a mist set sail.
And bells and kisses of the brave-eyed young
And the children with handkerchiefs flying.
It had set sail for happiness, majestic, embrowed,
And they groaned on the docks for sheer envy,
It had set sail for happiness, its stacks puffing
Idly, nor was there haste to set off
From the embracing bright ribbons of paper
Or the long regards of those blowing kisses
Parted by just so much distance of water
As the skirling long serpentines linked
With the silent weeping of farewelling hands.
There was after this (moon drowning in locks)
The ship's bells, the foghorns, the birds
As we ate sea biscuits and the porthole went pearl
And our hearts enraged by the pounding of engines
Throbbed just as hard
For countries more strange than those written in cloud
Or in those panes of the deep fens and fern
Beloved by childhood winters, held
In the long spying glasses of dream. . . .

FOUR

Her Spring Song

If I could live once more to see those flowers,
The daffodils and the bloodroot,
Those white, frail, long-petaled stars,
And a gang of crocuses,
Said the old woman with a clump
Of rosebushes she would plant,
Her hands thorn-pricked and scratched.

And hear that bird of sharp sweet song
Nor be deaf to its low cry
Nor blind to the flowers, I mean, both see
And hear the way I did when I
Danced as I walked
And had no need of any prop

Ah! And would do so now but that
Another wind blows
And I ache with the water over the stones
And where the wind tumbles the weirs
And the trouble of leaves scudded by airs
And ache with what each day
Must roll the sun around.

And have I lived too long
To keep enchanted eyes? And who was it said
That we improve with the years?
And yet to live without
The sense of the pulse of things,
No longer to keep time
To that pure animal tune,

To live without that. Not even a beast
Has to live so. And the work with the leaves,
The work with the earth,
The work, preparing for flowers,
To live, not knowing if

Because of what I do they'll thrive,
To have not even the imperative
Of sensitive plants that close
When light thins out and goes,

Impenitent upon my knees,
Hurt by the thing I love,
Not to pray to be possessed
Down under even death
By things as they were
When in their substance, firm and clear,
I thought I knew what all lived for,

And unwarily, unwarily,
Took so much to heart
It pulled the strings apart.

Spring Song II

And now my spring beauties,
Things of the earth,
Beetles, shards and wings of moth
And snail houses left
From last summer's wreck,
Now spring smoke
Of the burned dead leaves
And veils of the scent
Of some secret plant,

Come, my beauties, teach me,
Let me have your wild surprise,
Yes, and tell me on my knees
Of your new life.

How do my caged birds

How do my caged birds greet the day!
Unlike their jailor, who in prison bound
Creeps out of sleep to push the hours
An inchmeal pace toward that round mouth
That stops all pain and kill-care joy as well.
Freshly, as a plant gives leaves,
They give their song to new light every day,
They take the light for freedom and are gay,
Unlike their jailor, chained to a mindful time
Where every day connects since birth began
Its cunning cause and sequence. What free day
No longer tied to dying ones may bloom
For one who does time's task in time's wounds
Rehearsing for that metamorphosis
When flesh is grass a free bird sings upon?

Song for No Words

Usher the malcontents into the grove,
The withered shade of a grove.
Their godforsaken muse
Has closed the book of the rose
And now they have no tongue to tell
What they knew and knew so well
They swore they would know it forever.
They do not. For they awoke
On the other side of the rose.
What is the secret that they think
Only the thorns disclose?
O piercing nature of the rose!
Usher them into the grove
By the prospects of the moon.
Their muse has told them some such thing
As only a fool must learn.
And it is bitter to have to say
My godforsaken muse
Is out of humor with me,
And it is bitter to have to be
Tongueless now to tell
How it was or why
From every time-dishonored plot
The wolf and dog came back.
Usher them into the grove.
Their golden idols fell.
Let them pace livelong, nightly,
Between the boxwood walls and laurel.
Hands against their hearts pressed,
Let them weep and let them sing
Nasal, gusty chants to one
Who works in a little room.
May he stop their crying soon
With a very sandy rune.

For the Beauty of the Beau Monde

Being beautiful, all of your movements are,
And moments ride like ships into an eager place,
Likewise your charm, as if you knew
We'd love you as you love yourself.
Such confidence is better than disinterestedness
At making others think you're really kind.

And yet that charm's as if at variance
With all an idle beauty needs,
As if its glitter shone to prove to us
"You know how I love you" when actually—
But all we'd say of you is halfway guess.

Who know what you must be, and always smile
Who when you'd sigh would turn away
And if you'd frown would do so at your walls
When you're alone. But that is rare.
You like to spend your life in public ways.

And thus you live so cleverly we cry,
Your name is like a shot against the heart
When we surmise, although you may not say
(Only your eyes will give the truth away),
You play at what we cannot guess
As if you knew a way to counterfeit
A gaiety from something in the rift
Your beauty also bred from, parasite,
And play for us as if at heart
You lived for someone else we cannot guess,

The only one who will resist,
The only one you may not subjugate,
And who will keep your secrets quite intact,
For whom you need not learn your rules by rote
And need not smile nor dance,
And who's indifferent as death.

Poem

I open a door
And a moth comes in.
Welcome! I say, and depart,
Leaving the moth to my clothes
Or those snares
The spider will spin in the dark.
Will he grow fat on my wool
Or the spider upon his heart?
Creature of that blundering race
Of the horned brow and the furred face
There at my door, fluttering and crying
In the vegetable dews and the dark,
Like faces who haunt my night,
Ghost faces of my follies,
Crying my heart, my heart,
Let me in, let me in from the dark.
But I have put out the fire, my
Dears. Only the spiders wait.

A Note on Master Crow

A very portly crow
Black as a funeral
Waddled on my lawn
And cocked his head when he cawed
To answer other fellows down the road,
Leaving his bill ajar
For several minutes after.
Because the grass was new cut
He also stumbled over clumps of it.
The bird was prodigal
Of matters comical
And also of the humor saturnine,
Being so black and big
In the craw and wing,
So awkward and so hoarse,
So stately and so coarse,
And with such a look,
Upholstered like a davenport,
As of broad-backed bishop
Or of crook.

For a Day in the City

For spirit's sake I bought these flowers,
For spirit's sake, from off a cart
Drawn by a shaggy, black-shawled horse,
A festive Easter cart of red and white
Ungarnered lilies and the frail-stemmed, tall
Tulip with its flagon and its bowl
Of scalloped crimson and the clear samite.
Fresh with its perfumes and an Eastern loll
And cloudy with the young shoots of cool scent,
This wagon came as if it carried
A cloud upon its back or bed
Or in a cloud, back of my eyes,
Drove through my streets of heart elate.

The bandy-legged driver in his ease
Flourished like the lily in its leaves
As did that Jackanapes of hairy foot
Who pulled the farm of flowers at jogging rate,
As every blossom did beyond compare
At which I simply stood to stare
As if at chariots from the Caucasus.

My horse had tulips and his man lilies
And all survives, and all is not
Except the scarlet and the blue of stalk.
The air had rain and violets in its dark.
Came spring the champion in her coarse-wheeled cart
With news of leaves and letters and light love
Sprawled half-asleep upon the traveling ark.

Beside a Fall

Beside a fall there is a round wood pipe,
Capacious in dimension as a trunk,
That carries the dashing water to a mill.
But it is sprung with leaks. The water jets
In arcs and loops at almost every point.
The old cask is more sieve than case
To the delight of children and of me
Who come to watch the bursting seams
Of rusty iron-banded rings.
We like the little accident
Of fantastic ornament. . . .

French Country Circus

These are our players, the pony and the girl,
The wicked monkey and the panting dogs.
How quietly they come one afternoon!
The pony's eating grass just suddenly,
The monkey's sitting on his wooden house,
The dog beneath his wagon barks, and nanny baas
For mistress of the cold face and long hair
Who's telephoning in the *Poste*.
Already many come to stare
With grave eyes at the stars of this event.
What fresh surprise! to see them gathered there,
Installed so soon and busy right away!
Like nanny eating up a little tree
And pony with his bangs right in his eyes
Grazing the public grounds so seriously.
Although the monkey can't forget he's cross
The dog is lavish with his kissing tongue
When children come. And not a one seems nervous
Or seems tired. They take it, yes, within their stride.

At night they go through all their tricks,
The dogs through hoops, up ladders, and down slides,
The pony, dressed in bells, trots round the ring
So fast it makes you dizzy to the crack
Of the discourteous whip that eggs him on.
Perhaps it doesn't. He seems gay and calm.
The dogs with curly tails look on
And not a tongue that doesn't loll
When monkey rides him in a scarlet robe.

The girl is mistress of the animals.
The animals, so patient and adept,
Are masters of our feelings. That is just
As it should be had it been planned.
Tomorrow they'll be gone. I'll see them yet
Going through the towns "without a church,"

The laughter of small children and old men
Small compliment for which their mistress works
Although the animals don't seem to care.
They do not see themselves as charming or as good,
Indeed, they do not know their worth.
And if they did, how could we care as much?

If trees don't know what settles in them, Do birds know who roofs above them?

How into quite out of this
Came the birds!
Before the moonlight browsed
On the upland levels of the calm grass going gray
How they did on the evening tide
Settle together out of nowhere,
The wood dove and the slate-winged heron.
First was the wood dove, delicate-stately,
Hunched on a branch in buff dress with the marked
Breast showing, rooting under his wings
And plucking his brow,
And after that the large heron
Gliding in under his own light and power
To the same leafy square.
The translucency of two rarities met
In our tame woodland!
Neither of whom seemed to know nor to care
That the other was there,
Going about that supreme bird life
Of being sufficient everywhere
Each to his sphere,
Indifferent neighbors and fecund
In some most incurious union
Till the one tucked in and the other
Stooped down with deliberate air
To take the stones of the brook
Under his watchful care
And by dead reckoning snapped up a fish
That had leapt too far
Out of a stuff as confederate
And as unfathomable—
Unanimity beyond all unity,
Amity beyond all visibility—
The despair of our envy!

FIVE

Pays Perdu

There are those days, vivid and pure,
When everything dazzles, new found.
It is on days like this that we understand Eden,
Old worlds of the Golden Hours.
What is it. It is vigor, freshness,
A sense of the flags of day flying free,
It is commodious harmony,
We have fallen into some deepest relation
With self, the sense, and the world,
Being at rest strenuously
For all has form, moves with vivacious fluidity
Then nothing that seems extraneous
From the voices of bells caught, parted and cast away
To the blazings of twenty butterflies
Bemused by a stalk of blue flowers.
As if we had composed the day
With the slumbering unseen at the back of the mind
And we neither faint nor pale.
"When we are happy we have other names."

So it was on that day in the country
When my friend and I at large in a town
Fortified in its rock above a green river
(A champing and nervous force that had cut
Whole landscapes in two in its glacier course)
Started out at the height of noon
On the broad footpath by the river
Past gardens of garlic and artichoke
And groves of olive established in tiers.
It was in Provence and by the Var
In a country of vineyards and lizards
And the fragrance of many rough herbs in bloom
St. John's Eve, almost, and yet not come,
The perfect summer essence of the year.
Now, as we were along the way

We stopped to talk to a passerby
Proud to dispense the lore of the country,
A stranger herself, who spoke of a village
Far down the way, by the river, and of another
Far up in the mountains, hard if not impossible to find,
From which donkeys came down twice a week,
There being no road but a donkey track
And this track its only link with the world.
She herself had seen neither one
But she liked to think of them lurking
At the end of some straggling path. So did we,
And following her vague suggestion
That the one called Lacs, up in the mountains,
Was somewhere *down* and then *up*, set out,
Larky and confident.

This much we knew, that in an old country
That holds many bones, where life has been hard,
Where much dust of the nightingale
Is mixed with the dust of poppies
And the stubborn roots of valerian, and all
The medicinal sages,
That in an old country crossed by centuries of animals and men
There are many paths possible to take.
Foxes and dogs made them first,
Horses and donkeys succeeded.
Then the paths were secured, steps were cut out,
Walls were erected.
An old country is crisscrossed with paths,
Shortcuts to the crest of a mountain.
Look at some track up the terraces
Where the olive trees doze
And you ought to know it is going somewhere.

2

And of the three-hour walk in the blaze of day
Up the snail-spiraling way of the rough country—
Scrub oak and stone—
And the three vertigoes when the path fell sheer

By the cliffside straight to the river
And there was white limestone dust and a chalky glare
Blinding—
                    and the heat—   till we cooked—
And knew the beginnings of thirst—
                              and were lost—
Or deceived by a choice of paths
So retraced our steps to a farm
Where the goat-faced owner who had been asleep
Shouted down from the upper-story window
(After his dogs had barked themselves hoarse)
That if we wanted to visit a "pays perdu"
Take the fork back there to the left—

And of the way up by hawk's beak and claw
By rock horn and fang and skull,
By the death's-head grin of the spurred headlands
As the path twisted inland,
Broad enough at times for two donkeys
But losing us in the basil and marjolain
And long ceased the groves of the flickering olive
The derelict houses and storing sheds
As we climbed on past a pinewood
The sun glinting on its tufts and its cones
And blanching the rock formations.
And into what were we going, leaving the river,
That broad boulevard, that viable thread,
To go back and into the crowded interior,
Crowded, that is, with trees and more rock and many small
                                          mountains
That engendered, for all that we knew, cockatrices. . . .
(And at one turning in a medley of rubble
Meeting a child, a little girl,
Carrying a basket that had a cloth cover
Who was so startled on seeing us and hearing us speak
That we thought her a mute, she taking so long to answer,
And then in a voice as if rusty from long disuse.)

This the first stage: after that, more declivities,
More mournful ostentation of rock as we climbed

And knew thirst and passed through more deadlands
Meeting the sense of the torture of time.

History is time and it assailed us, the sight of those signs of that
static tempest that had once pressed forth those needles of stone
that once again met us, and the swirled water-marked rippled bad-
rock effects across yet another harsh breach in earth's crust cut by
the Var's ravening tributary.

And if music is the energy of time, immensely loading some quarter-
hour with the compressed violence of meanings too numerous,
shades too elusive striving against the iron gates and in one crazed
hurl achieving the leap, so the ever continuing variations of new
fantasies of rock made us laggard. Impressed us? Pressed on, op-
pressed us. Ejaculations of rock pipes with crumbling flutings!
Perches for birds or stylites, grotesque and badly botched Byzantine
pillars!

And our weak shoes half in ribbons from so much pulverizing by
                                                              pebbles.
And we streaked with sweat and the taste of much dryness.
Grown over by land, by what we had seen,
Bruised by the stones white with dust and pollen,
Burnt by the sun in a mirth
Of the incurable singing of the nightingale.
For we had spied on the bird in a round bush
Though that was below, near the river.
Up here, in the miles inland, bees followed us
But not that Greek thrush. Here it was birdless,
Wildness in waste,
And the distintegrating black schist,
Porphyry headlands, beetling and angled. . . .

And then by a turn, roofs!
And our drouth drank of the cordial.
For here would be douce water, casks of it, vats,
And we dreamed up the café, for what town was without one,
Where we would sit, steeped in mineral water,
Citron pressé, and after that, *café*
Before we'd begin on water again.

But as a mountain is never the same
When you are traveling toward it,
Presenting at each turn another view of its one hundred faces
And as space itself is as deceiving,
So we lost that prospect, another turning swallowed it up,
We jogged on, thinking of donkeys
And what kind of people were these who lived so far inland?
And who could ever take over these mountains?
Dense earth resisted, hail to its lordship
That would thrust us out of its holdings!

Nor by more turnings did the roofs swim back
Although we came to a bridge
Where the path broadened into a road.
Now the sky was staring with a sudden stark blue
Over the flank of a new mountain
And two or three paths coiled before us.
All was less wild, we had modulated
Into what might have been at one time subdued
By the plough, though forgotten by now,
A table of land half pasture,
And we went this way and that
Attempting to skirt the shape of the land
And was it a mirage? we half joked,
Had our thirst started up a fever so soon?
Wasn't it an hour ago we had seen
The tiptilting roofs? Into what had they gone?

Then suddenly a wheatfield
And a gulley of stones and a sharp hill
Up which we stumbled into storm blue,
The sky full of violent, crazed blue,
And a wind rolling in the trees
By a haycock shaped like a loaf of bread
And truly the roofs and surely the water!
And we running now across the shorn field
Till we came to the first faces of houses.
The field rode up to their windows
And the shutters on them were closed

And the silence could not be more unstirred
Until we called out and black and white doves
Started up with a creak of wings
And we called again. But where were the people?
Was it inhabited by black and white doves or pigeons?

3

And we went around a corner, if you can call it that, between one
house with its roof fallen in and one whole one and into a court-
yard with lime trees in bloom and three or four houses across the
way and saw a woman, wearing a man's peaked hat and a man's
shoes, running with a pack of hay on her back, and a woman in a
big straw hat and three dogs that came at us snarling and as the
wind buffeted the lime trees and the crazed blue grew stalwart we
saw *this* was the town but *there* was the water running from a pipe's
mouth into a tub. What a stir! for if we were apparitions to them
they were not less to us, and the dogs barking for all they were
worth till a man called them off and one who had been willing to
hurl himself at our throats now wagging his tail as we explained
how long we had been walking and—THIRST! And he pointed
triumphantly to what they had an abundance of.

Then we rather crazy there at the tub, filling our hands with
water . . .
And my friend lying prone and drinking from the pipe's mouth.

While bundles of hay kept flying past us on the backs of the man
and woman and the one in a straw hat calling out in a language
we had never heard to which was added the delirium of birds just
before rain—swallows springing out of nowhere to shriek and to
skirl and a swooping by pigeons while a battery of crows cawed by.

And as the storm sky humped down I running out in the unearthly
blue to the "other side" of the town . . . which was likewise a field
that stretched off to a mountain. But more. Much more. Where I
stood was before the very birth of a chaos of definable forms. So
here they were, put down in a lull, the last lull between peaks.
Since to the "back" or the north stretched that beginning of the
one thousand wrinkled circus-tent tops.

Till the rain came down in a blithe bluster of spears and the air was so freshened with the breath of all that seems good that the rain froze and we were peppered with a fine shot of hail and took refuge under a shed until the man who had been carrying hay asked us into his house.

And we saw, going in, a bright blue postbox at the side of his door

And we went into the first black room
Filled with blossoms of the lime tree in gunnysacks
And loose on the floor and on a table, and into the kitchen
With an iron stove and scraps in a pan on the floor for a dog
And the woman in the peaked hat was there
With eyes that ate up her face
Nodding to us and smiling but sitting away where we could not
see her,
Sitting away in a corner like a bird mewed up,
And her husband eager to do the talking
With the stub of a burnt-out cigarette
In the corner of his mouth like a sore,
Slight and not young,
His beret jammed tight to his head. . . .
And he wanted to know just how we had happened to come
Because where they were, few did.
And was it true that the donkeys went down
Twice a week or more? we asked.
About that, he was vague. Yes, he had donkeys
And when the wheat was cut—
We understood then that truly at times
The donkeys went down with produce
And returned with provisions.
And we heard of the postman who came twice a week
Five miles by the ravines and the gorges
Because there was a postbox and it was the law
Whether there was mail or not—
And of a teacher who also came
Twice a week for the one child left.
So. They were not forgotten. He voted.
And they had gone to war,
Two families left now, and one child.
And Lacs had been named for a lake

77

That had disappeared so long ago
Not even his father's grandfather had seen it
And this house—almost as old!
They had had sheep till the shepherd had left
And years ago there had been hundreds
Sheep, that is, with their shepherds
Up from the valley to stay the whole summer.
In his father's day there had been horse roads
Now grown over, and the houses for lizards. . . .

He was quick and gentle in the way he spoke
Wearing a cigarette that would not stay lit—
Steadfastly refusing our own.
No animal earth-spirit, weathered and contrary,
But equable, civil.
We felt that it pleased him to talk
Especially of the heroical postman
And the thistle hearts that his mother cooked
For the good that it did them
Like that herb that she swore if you put in your shoe
You could walk miles and never get tired
But he used to walk to the valley half the nights of the week.
Youth was his herb.

And of what else we talked about . . .
As the lime blossoms trembled in the next room
Where a wild bee stumbled and throbbed. . . .
Of the grass fire that made the bees leave
(When they kept bees) and bees won't come back
To a place that's burned
And the mushrooms and snails that came after rain
And one time, long after midnight
The chapel bell rang and rang
And whether the wind or an animal rang it,
For the rope had worked loose, they never knew.

And the strange Lacs stirred for us
As the lime blossoms trembled in the next room
When he peopled the sides of hill,
Had carts jolting by that took wheat to a mill,

78

Humors of barnyards—the Gaulois cock crowing,
Goats with their niddering voices, vigors and motion
And all the desires we connect with action
Before the roofs fell and the field mice came in. . . .
And how is it, we wanted to say,
As you gather the lime flowers to store or to sell,
Though it take the whole heart do you labor
So close to the nerve and burn
Of the great stars in the stillness
That is as strong as sound. . . .

While he told of the fête, just at this time of year,
Of John the Baptist when a handful of men
Would go into the mountains to a "desert" there
And stay for two nights, fasting and praying,
And on the night they came back
Everyone going to meet them
With flutes and fifes and the moaning procession. . . .
And yes, there was a chapel just over the meadow
And what the woman spoke who wore the straw hat
Was Provençal. . . .

And the rain had long since stopped
And it was time to go
And he would not accept our cigarettes
Though there was the thought we would send him a postcard
If nothing else for the sake of the postman
And we said our farewells and his wife smiled back
With that look not to be pitied, nor understood
And out into Lacs again
We saw what we had not seen before—
Two houses stood sound and whole
The rest toppling like hollyhocks
Or topless, with a tree gushing from a door.
We saw how secluded and secret,
How inward a crumbling thing looks,
The eyeless ruins or the three-cornered ones,
Time not running away as in music
Nor the instant lit up with energy
But grinding and pulverizing with an idiot's patience

The rock foundations.
And it would not be stopped, it would be
As the wind and the weather would have it,
It would go down to the soundless possession
Of the rash bugles of morning glory.

And what can we do, said my friend,
Can we send them something, a gift.
They have given up, they are dying,
They are going down with the place
And this—she waved her hand
For we were passing the fields again
And the same big birds beating up—
Makes them indifferent. They are too much lulled
By the lull in the mountains.
And the fields swelling to the horns of green hills.
It could not be more beautiful
Nor the quality of the way it lay
In between old hills and young mountains
Could not be met again
Nor the quality of the silence
That we would have in our ears for days.
And we passed the haycock and found the path
Leaving that phantasmal space
As if drawn for the soul to dream in
For which, once we left it, there could be no maps.
"Pays perdu!" said the goat-faced man,
And *lacs* also meant a snare made with strings
To catch birds with, as we understood—
Oh terror and beauty!

And who was to say that their souls were held
In the space here in between mountains
As the thyme and the rosemary perfume the shadows
That the great bodies cast down from their crowns?
And who was to speak of mountain flowers
That can blossom only after snow and deep frost,
Their colors intensified by the rare air,
Resisting the aridity, the cold nights, the poverty of soil,
Indeed, these very deprivations, that struggle

Being necessary for their perfection of a few days?
It was not to say this
                              in the great light
And the forms aloof over the serenity of ruins.

And we took the long way down,
Loping along it easily in the cool of the day,
Not tormented by thirst,
As the small perfumes of earth began to be freed,
The dry-shod ferny gusts,
And shawls of blue shadow cast
On the pale green of dented slopes
Whole peaks in shadow
And whole landscapes in cloud—
"Those intricate thoughts, those elaborate emotions—"
Where at the converging of four peaks
A cloud makes a fifth.

Morality

Observe the Roman Forum; turn away.
That pasture of cold time has had its day.
Smile as you say this who will be
Dust when these stones still mark the Sacred Way.